Allah
KNOWS
EVERYTHING
الله بِكُلّ شَيْءٍ عَلِيم
Green Fig
Proud Muslim Kids
AF266554

Allah knows my name.

اللَّهُ يَعْلَمُ ٱسْمِي.

Allah knows my thoughts.

اللَّهُ يَعْلَمُ أَفْكَارِي.

Allah knows where I hide my toys.
اللَّهُ يَعْلَمُ أَيْنَ أُخَبِّئُ أَغْرَاضِي.

Allah knows where the ant
walks under the ground.

اللَّهُ يَعْلَمُ أَيْنَ تَمْشِي
كُلُّ نَمْلَةٍ تَحْتَ ٱلْأَرْضِ.

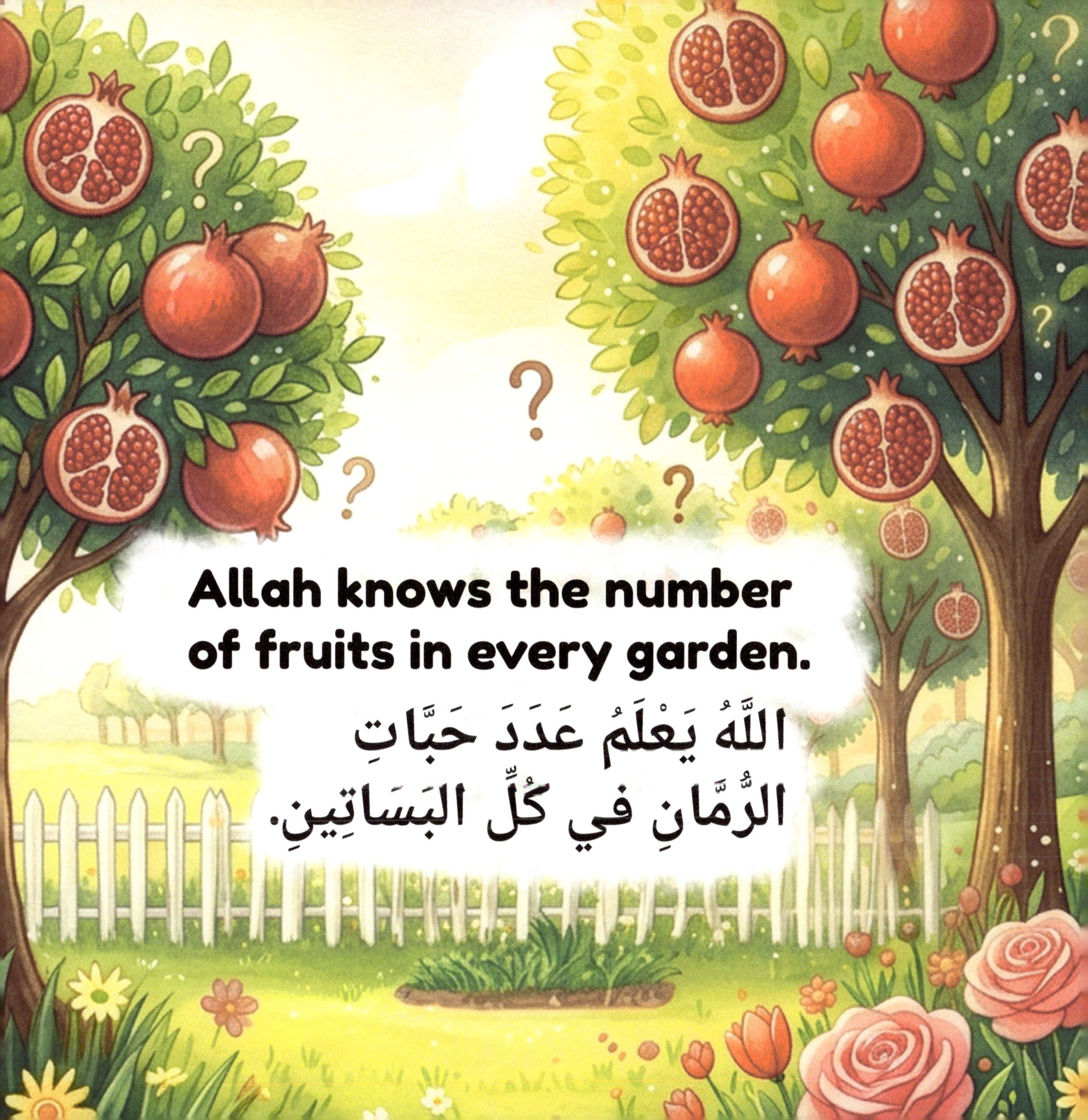

Allah knows the number of fruits in every garden.
اللَّهُ يَعْلَمُ عَدَدَ حَبَّاتِ الرُّمَّانِ في كُلِّ البَسَاتِينِ.

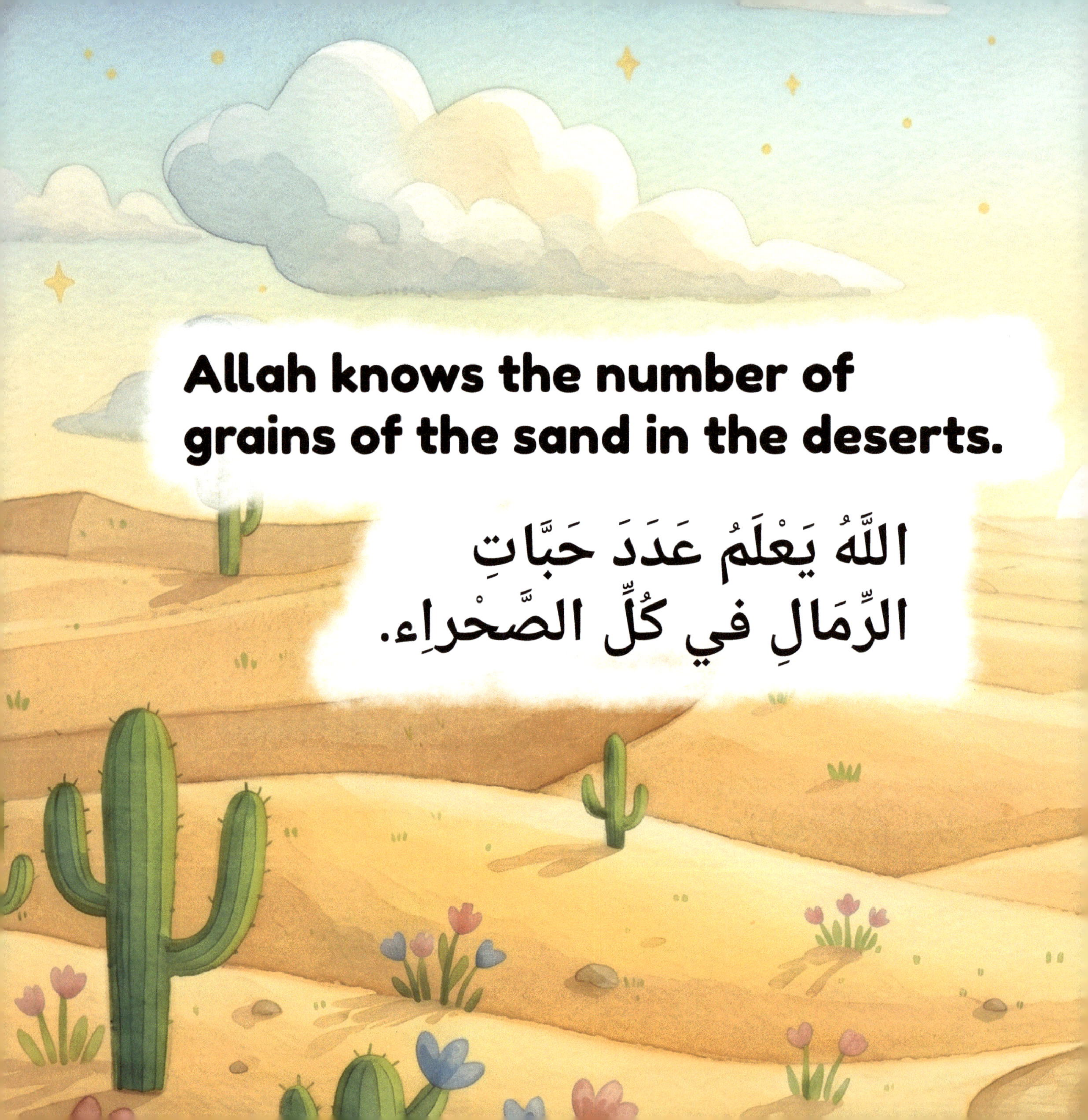

Allah knows the number of grains of the sand in the deserts.

اللَّهُ يَعْلَمُ عَدَدَ حَبَّاتِ الرَّمَالِ فِي كُلِّ الصَّحْرَاءِ.

Allah knows what is hidden in the ground.

اللَّهُ يَعْلَمُ مَا هُوَ مَخْفِيٌّ فِي ٱلْأَرْضِ.

All knows what is in the
depth of the sea.
اللَّهُ يَعْلَمُ مَا فِي أَعْمَاقِ ٱلْبَحْرِ.

Allah knows what happened before I was born.

اللَّهُ يَعْلَمُ مَاذَا حَدَثَ قَبْلَ أَنْ أُولَدَ.

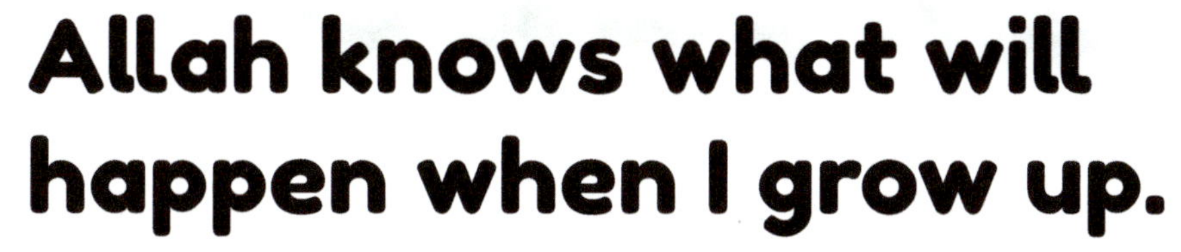

Allah knows what will happen when I grow up.

اللَّهُ يَعْلَمُ مَاذَا سَيَحْدُثُ بَعْدَ أَنْ أَكْبُرَ.

Allah knows everything.
اللَّهُ يَعْلَمُ كُلَّ شَيْء.

I Love Allah who knows everything.

أُحِبُّ ٱللَّهَ الْعَالَمُ بِكُلِّ شَيْءٍ.

قال الله تعالى:
﴿ وَهُوَ بِكُلِّ شَيْءٍ عَلِيمٌ ﴾
سورة الأنعام: ﴿١٠١﴾

The Proud Muslim Kids series by Green Fig books is designed to engagingly teach youngsters basic concepts of Islam in a way that speaks to their hearts and minds. Each book in the series is crafted by a staff of qualified educators, writers, illustrators, parents and children. Not only is the Proud Muslim Kids series designed to supplement the early childhood and elementary Islamic curriculum, it isa great addition to any school or home library. Covering a wide variety of topics such as the Five Pillars of Islam, Islamic culture, and Islamic history, parents and children will return to these books and enjoy them together time and time again.

Publisher: Green Fig
Pennsylvania, USA
gogreenfig.com
info@gogreenfig.com
Allah Knows Everything
ISBN: 978-1-953836-97-7